Original title:
Life's Big Questions and Tiny Answers

Copyright © 2025 Creative Arts Management OÜ
All rights reserved.

Author: Eleanor Prescott
ISBN HARDBACK: 978-1-80566-168-9
ISBN PAPERBACK: 978-1-80566-463-5

The Depths of Everyday Wonder

Why does toast always land face down?

And where's my sock that disappeared in town?

Is it possible to know why the cat meows?

Or why I can't remember what I just found?

Why do we trip on the things in our way?

Is my phone trying to steal my last hooray?

And why do my plants grow just to say 'bye'?

As long as they're fed, do they truly care why?

What's the meaning of all my lost keys?

If I find them, will I unlock all my dreams?

Why do I find joy in the most silly things?

In laughter, is hidden what wisdom still brings?

Echoes of Answer and Inquiry

What's in that box that sits by my door?

Is it cookies or a mystery I should explore?

Why can't ducks ever be properly aligned?

Are they just quacking, or is there more we can find?

Why do socks vanish when laundry's a chore?

They carpet the floor, but still want to soar.

How can my coffee be colder than ice?

I swear just a minute, I checked it twice!

Is the cat judging me while I eat my lunch?

Does he think my sandwich needs more of a crunch?

Why does the cat act like he owns the place?

Maybe in his world, I'm just a disgrace!

The Journey to the Heart of Being

Do I really need eight types of cheese?

Or is that just a lavish way to please?

Why does it rain when I'm wearing white?

The universe surely has a sense of spite!

What if I told you the mirror lies back?

It's just a reflection, a sneaky little hack.

Why does my dog think the mailman's a foe?

Perhaps he's just bored and needs a good show!

Why do we ponder on things that confuse?

Like why is it hard to find matching shoes?

What's the secret behind all this fuss?

Maybe it's joy in life's playful discuss!

A Universe in a Grain of Sand

A grain of sand at the beach,
Holds galaxies within its reach.
Why is the sky so very blue?
Maybe it's just a big ol' preview.

Can crabs hold secret meetings?
Do they discuss their little beatings?
Or is the tide their grand excuse,
To dance around without a ruse?

Secrets Beneath the Surface

What's hiding in my cup of tea?
A universe of thoughts, you see.
Maybe I'll sip and test my fate,
Or let the leaves just meditate.

Do fishes ever get tired of swimming?
Or, like us, find joy in the dimming?
Perhaps they dream of flying high,
Or plotting a splash to the sky.

Tiny Revelations in Vastness

A star fell once, or did it wink?
Must be deep thoughts, don't you think?
When ants carry crumbs to their home,
Are they just shopping or having a roam?

Do clouds ever argue over the sun?
"It's my turn!" "No, I'm way more fun!"
Or do they just float and argue in jest?
Finding humor in not knowing the rest?

The Essence of Fleeting Moments

Tick-tock goes the sneaky clock,
Reminding me to take a walk.
But what if I stop to smell the cheese?
Perhaps there's wisdom in the breeze.

Do socks dream of a missing mate?
Or simply laugh at their own fate?
In mismatched world, they find some glee,
Wearing their stripes proud, happily free.

The Fabric of Fragile Dreams

Why does my toast always land down?
A mystery wrapped in buttered frown.
Do socks disappear when I'm not near?
Or do they just vanish, fueled by fear?

The moon's made of cheese, or so they say,
But why do I crave it in the light of day?
If wishes were fishes, I'd swim in my bowl,
Then I'd just fish for a whimsy role.

Searching for Clarity in the Fog

Why do I trip over every thin air?
It's like gravity thinks it's having a stare.
If time flies like pigeons, where do they land?
Perhaps in a park where they play in the sand?

Why do I count sheep to fall into sleep?
Dreams wrapped in mumbles feel big, but they're cheap.
If my goldfish had wings, would it try to soar?
Or just float around, proclaiming, 'No more!'

Tiny Questions from a Bigger World

If aliens watch me, am I the main show?
Do they munch on popcorn while taking a low?
What if my cat's plotting a feline coup?
I swear that she nodded when I left the room too!

Can I teach spiders to knit me a hat?
Or is it just safer to stick with a cat?
How do you measure a laugh or a sigh?
With giggles like feathers that flutter and fly?

The Heartbeat of Questions Unasked

Is cereal a soup? Now that's the thing,
Should I be concerned, or simply just sing?
Why do we park on driveways and drive on the street?
Does this confusion come from life's quirky beat?

Do butterflies know how lovely they appear?
Or do they just flutter, not caring, my dear?
If ducks played chess, would it be a draw?
Or would they quack loudly, 'What's the law?'

Glimmers of Insight

Why do socks always disappear,
As if they've vanished without a fear?
I ponder deeply in the night,
Only to find one in plain sight.

Is it fate or cosmic jest,
That keeps our answers on a quest?
I trip on thoughts both big and small,
Laughing as they tumble and fall.

Why does toast always land face down?
Could it be, I'm cursed in this town?
Each crumb and mishap leads to cheer,
As logic drips like melted beer.

So let's embrace the silly quest,
For tiny truths that we jest.
In giggles wrapped, we'll try to find,
The strange way answers play with our mind.

The Pursuit of Elusive Truths

What's the meaning of this dance,
Of juggling life without a chance?
The more I seek, the less I know,
As silly thoughts steal the show.

Why do cats ignore my calls,
As if I'm small, and they stand tall?
They glare at me with utmost pride,
While I just slip and slide.

Is there a map for this odd race,
Or just a mirror to our face?
I laugh at riddles tossed about,
In a world that sometimes seems in doubt.

So let's toast to questions so absurd,
And find the truth in every word.
In the chaos, let's take a peek,
At tiny answers that make us speak.

Quiet Revelations

Why do we chase the ticking clock,
As if it hides some secret rock?
Time slips past, a sneaky thief,
While we wrestle with sweet belief.

Do plants really listen to our woes,
Or is that just what the gardener knows?
With every whisper from our heart,
They perk up, playing their part.

Why do we laugh when we should cry,
Using humor to get us by?
Each chuckle hides a little grace,
In the frantic, madcap race.

So let's sit back with our tea,
And laugh at what will never be.
In silence, tiny truths will reminisce,
With a wink, we find our bliss.

Searching for Stars in the Fog

Why does wisdom hide in clouds,
While silliness stands out in crowds?
I squint and search, my head in space,
But all I find is a silly face.

Is there a guide for this wild ride,
Or just a friend who'll sit beside?
I wander through the misty haze,
Stumbling on thoughts that often graze.

Why do we trip on words so light,
Yet get weighed down by the dark night?
In the chill, we laugh and dance,
As stars come out to join the chance.

So take my hand, let's chase the glow,
Through tangled thoughts that ebb and flow.
We'll catch a giggle, find it neatly,
In the fog of questions, sweet and fleet.

When Questions Dance with Doubts

Why does the sun rise with such flair?
Is it aiming to catch a selfie there?
Do trees gossip when the wind blows?
Or do they just sway and share their woes?

When is it too late for a midnight snack?
Is that why the fridge holds the attack?
What if socks have a secret club?
Dog ears pricked, they heard the grub!

Can you tickle a fish or is it a lie?
What if they giggle while swimming by?
Do clouds play tag up high in the sky?
Or do they just float, and that's why they sigh?

What do ants think of our grand parade?
"Look at those giants," they often have said.
If questions had legs, would they run away?
Leaving us here for another day!

Answers in the Breeze

Why do bicycles have to be two?
Couldn't one wheel have done it too?
Is laughter the best kind of cheer?
Or does chocolate hold the crown so dear?

What if stars are just shiny bugs?
Sticking heads out for warm bear hugs?
Do fish want to swim through the air?
Or are they just happy with water to spare?

If cats had jobs, would they be CEOs?
Or just take naps with a side of prose?
What's the real reason for squirrel chatter?
Secrets or just to see who's fatter?

When the wind whispers through your hair,
Is it a secret or just a dare?
Answers drift like feathers and leaves,
One day they'll land, and that's when we grieve!

The Small Clarity in Chaos

In the eye of a storm, is it quiet there?
Or just a moment before the wild flare?
Can pancakes really bring world peace?
Or are they just breakfast? A sweet lease?

Why do dogs chase their own silly tails?
Is it to uncover their wild, doggy trails?
Do crickets sing for joy or for fright?
Or just to impress the stars at night?

Can you scare a shadow by running fast?
Or does it have fun, watching you gasp?
When jellybeans dance in a jar,
Do they dream of candy bars and a car?

Is a wink from the moon a friendly sign?
Or just a twinkle from a celestial mind?
Amidst the chaos, do giggles rise?
For small strokes of joy, in the world of sighs!

Ponderings on the Edge of Time

If clocks could talk, would they tick-tock wise?
Or would they just gossip about our goodbyes?
Is time a thief or a constant friend?
Or just a loop that has no end?

What do dreams taste like—sweet or sour?
Do they growl during our sleeping hour?
When do we actually know we've arrived?
Is it when the coffee keeps us revived?

Can shoes hold secrets of where we've been?
Or are they just waiting to feel the sheen?
What if whispers hold the key to truth?
Hidden in giggles of innocent youth?

Can silence dance, or does it only stand?
Waiting for madness to give it a hand?
On the edge of time, with questions galore,
We dive into laughter, forever to explore!

Dances of Destiny

When the cat walks, what does it mean?
The dog just shrugs, if you know what I mean.
Is the universe a grand old dance?
Or just random steps, with no second chance?

Will the cupcake fall if left to bake?
Does it make a sound or is it just fake?
The eagle soared, the rabbit hopped
Maybe it's all just a jig we dropped.

So ask the stars, they twinkle and tease,
But who really knows? They just do as they please.
In the end, let's all wear our hats,
And dance on the floor with the funky cats!

For destiny's just a game of charades,
Two left feet and a couple of fades.
We laugh and we glide, in a jig or a stumble,
'Cause wise are those who know how to fumble!

The Stillness of Uncertainty

Why is the fridge hum like a bee?
Asking ourselves, 'What will I be?'
A potato today, a french fry tomorrow,
Is it worth the weight or just full of sorrow?

In the great cosmic web of 'maybe' and 'might',
My coffee's too cold, should I sip or take flight?
A pigeon just pooped, what does this reveal?
Am I the one standing or just an ideal?

We question with glee, like a kid with a kite,
Should I plunge into dark or bask in the light?
With answers so tiny, we giggle and jest
Perhaps being clueless is actually the best!

So here's to the void, where nonsense reigns,
To sell lemonade while it sometimes rains.
You may not be sure, but that's quite alright,
We just might find fun in this uncertain flight!

Fleeting Thoughts in a Boundless Sea

A thought hit me like a rogue wave,
If I'm just a fish, what will I crave?
Should I seek treasure or swim with the sharks?
Or hang with the kelp, catching some sparks?

In the ocean of dreams, I'm just a flake,
Drifting along for my own piece of cake.
The octopus ponders as it changes its hue,
'What's the meaning of it all? Or just this view?'

Seashells whisper secrets, they laugh and they tease,
Maybe the ocean just likes to freeze.
With every wave, another thought fades,
Perhaps here's where the real fun parades!

So grab a surfboard, let's ride with the tide,
Who needs answers? Just jump on, take a glide!
In a sea of confusion, we'll float with a smile,
And make silly memories, if only a while!

Reflections in a Polished Stone

In a stone so smooth, what do I see?
A flash of a moment, or just a cup of tea?
If rocks could talk, oh what would they tell?
Funny stories of giants and how they fell.

Do stones get bored just sitting around?
Waiting for humans to kick them or ground?
With every crack, is a tale to unfold,
Maybe they laugh at the things we're sold.

'Truth is a pebble lying in the sand,'
Said the wise old boulder, or so I've planned.
But who really knows? I'll make a joke,
As I skip over puddles, and drink from a Coke!

So let's cherish the moments, both big and small,
For in polished stones, it's the giggles that call.
With a wink and a nod to the cosmos above,
We'll toss our thoughts gently, just like a dove!

Glimmers in the Abyss of Thought

Why bother with the universe's scheme?
A sandwich makes the perfect dream.
Stars may twinkle with lots of might,
But who needs them when cheese is right?

Questions swirling like dust in air,
Where's my sock? It's still not there!
Philosophers ponder, but I just know,
I can't find my keys, where did they go?

Wandering minds in a deep abyss,
Must be something I really miss.
Thoughts as jumbled as spaghetti strings,
Yet here I am, just wanting wings.

In the end, it's all just fun,
Like shooting arrows, aiming at none.
Throw in a laugh, and all's just right,
Twirling 'round the absurdity of night.

The Quest for Certainty in a Sea of Doubt

I once sought truth with a map in hand,
But the directions were written in sand.
Mountains of doubt, rivers of fear,
I stopped for ice cream, said, 'Who needs seer?'

Is the sky really blue? I can't confirm,
But the taste of chocolate? That's the real term.
I asked a cat for a pithy reply,
It just blinked at me, oh my, oh my!

With every tick of the clock, I wade,
Through puddles of questions, I'm feeling frayed.
Yet in the chaos that muddles my brain,
I laugh at the circus, quite insane!

As I drift in this ocean, no life vest found,
I'll dance to the rhythm of questions unbound.
Let's toast to the seekers, the wanderers too,
With a slice of pizza, that's my view!

Answers Beneath a Starry Canopy

Under a sky that whirls and twirls,
I contemplate the mystery of pearls.
Why do I trip over my own two feet?
I guess there's no answer, but it's kinda neat!

Stars glimmer like foil on my favorite wrap,
I gaze and ponder—did I forget a map?
Constellations argue over old debates,
While I just munch on snack-filled plates.

Lost in wonder, I scratch my head,
Thinking of the questions I never said.
Can I float on clouds, ride a rainbow too?
But first, where's that taco I dream to chew?

So here's to the answers hiding in sight,
Cloaked in slapstick, laughter is light.
With each little giggle, I slyly confess,
The tiny answers are often the best!

The Journey Through a Thousand Whys

Why does the toast always hit the floor?
I've pondered this deeply, and still want more.
With each crumb that flutters past my shoe,
I question if gravity has a say too!

A thousand whys chase me like a breeze,
If pigeons can fly, why not bumblebees?
I ask my cactus for its wise decree,
It just stood there, silent as can be.

With donuts and coffee, I fuel my quest,
At this rate, I'll need a vacation, at best!
Each whimsy wonder tickles my brain,
While I sit on my couch, dressed only in grain.

So here's to the voyage of silly delight,
Where questions play tag in the dead of night.
Let's laugh at the mysteries, big and small,
And dance through the nonsense, embracing it all!

The Art of Wondering

Why do socks always disappear?
Is there a sock thief, I fear?
Do clouds wear hats as they float by?
Or is that just a dream, oh my?

Do ants hold meetings on the ground?
Discussing snacks that can be found?
Can grass bend down just to say hi?
I'd join their chat, if I could fly!

What's the reason for a rooster's crow?
Is it to let the world just know?
Or perhaps it's just a wake-up call
To remind us all that time won't stall?

Is the moon just a big cheese wheel?
Or does it have a special feel?
Could it be a giant's lost delight?
Making wishes on it each night?

Small Answers to Great Mysteries.

Why does ice cream taste so sweet?
Especially when it's on a seat?
Do we eat it just for the fun?
Or does it hide from the sun?

If fish can swim, can birds all float?
Or is that just a silly quote?
Why do dreams escape our grasp?
It's like they wear a clever mask!

How does toast always land buttered side?
Is it destiny, or just pride?
And why do cats sit on laptops?
As if they're kings, with no stops!

Is a banana really a fruit?
Or just a long, yellow suit?
What's with the sound of a honking goose?
Is it just asking for some juice?

Searching the Stars for Simple Truths

Do stars wink at us from afar?
Or are they just quirky, bizarre?
Could a planet be made of cheese?
Asking Earth, could you pass the peas?

Will aliens bring us their best dish?
Or just ask us for a strange wish?
What if the Milky Way's a huge shake?
With cosmic sprinkles for our take?

Is gravity just a pulled-in hug?
Or a dance that's a little snug?
Do comets have tails, just for fun?
Or are they shy, on the run?

Why do we look up in the night?
Hoping to find a sign of light?
What if the sky is simply blue?
And the stars are just peeking through?

Whispers of Existence

Why does a sneeze make us say bless?
Is it magic, or just a guess?
What do plants think as they grow tall?
Do they hear our jokes at all?

Are the clouds just marshmallows in flight?
Making the day feel light and bright?
What happens when we all close new doors?
Do they gossip about us, with roars?

If I talk to my fridge, is it sane?
Does it hear me, or feel no pain?
And when will we find socks that mate?
Or maybe it's fun to keep them late?

Why do we chase dreams like lost socks?
Is the key found in paradox?
Could smiling at chaos bring us peace?
Or just more questions that increase?

The Paradox of Simplicity

Why does a spoon bend light?
Yet I can't find the end of my plight.
I search for answers, oh what a task,
When all I need is a simple flask.

Why do we trip on our own two feet?
Look for wisdom in chocolate sweet.
The questions grow like laundry piles,
But the truth wears mismatched styles.

A wise old sage once said with glee,
"Complexity's just a silly spree."
But here I am with thoughts in a whirl,
And a hangnail that sets my world in a twirl.

So if you ponder with cumbersome thought,
Remember, simplicity can't be bought.
Just laugh at the mess, and take a seat,
For simplicity's wrapped in your favorite treat.

Unraveling Threads of Existence

Threads of being knot and weave,
Yet I'm missing my favorite sleeve.
Is existence just a pie in the sky?
Or maybe a donut that makes us sigh?

With each strand that I try to pull,
I find my thoughts increasingly dull.
Am I the shoe or the shoelace?
Does it matter—who's keeping the pace?

Explaining the universe is a tall task,
But it sure is fun if you just wear a mask.
Pretend to know while you sip your tea,
You may just become the next mystery!

Fear not the wild cosmic ballet,
Just dance on by in your own unique way.
Threads may tangle, but here's the glee:
Even knotted yarn can create jubilee!

Minuscule Truths in Vastness

In a universe so broad and vast,
I ponder my lunch, 'Will this last?'
Are secrets hiding between the stars?
Or is it just soup in old jars?

I asked a rock, but it stayed mute,
Glued to the ground and missing a suit.
So I turned to my feline friend,
And wondered if she'd ever comprehend?

Tiny truths under the grand moonlight,
Like finding a penny that feels quite right.
With every whim, I discover anew,
That meaning sometimes comes with a mew.

So as I float on this boat of thought,
In seas of questions that can't be caught,
I'll laugh at the vastness, sip my brew,
And know the tiniest truths can carry you through.

Navigating the Ocean of Inquiry

On a ship of questions, I set to sail,
With a cargo of dreams and a bottle of ale.
What lies ahead in this vast expanse?
Do waves dance to the rhythm of chance?

I chart my course with a compass of fun,
Though it usually points at the nearest bun.
Each wave of thought brings a chuckle and nudge,
While I munch on my sandwich, it gives me a grudge.

Navigating life can be quite absurd,
Like swimming with a flightless bird.
But as I cast lines into the blue,
I find treasures in questions I didn't pursue.

So here's to the ocean, vast and wide,
With curiosities as my only guide.
Just steer with humor, don't take it too hard,
For even the best maps may leave you marred!

The Quest for Meaning in Fleeting Moments

Why do ducks quack in a row?
Do they think they'll win a show?
Is it wisdom or just a game?
The answers are never the same.

Should I count sheep to find some sleep?
Or write a novel that runs too deep?
What if my plot just fizzles out?
I'll toss it like ice cream, no doubt!

Why do socks always lose their mate?
My laundry seems to hold a fate,
Of mismatched pairs and lonely hearts,
Smart socks must know how to play parts.

In a world of chaos, where's the key?
Is it hidden in a cup of green tea?
Perhaps there's wisdom in mugs we sip,
Just don't let spills ruin the trip!

Petals of Inquiry

Why do flowers bloom and fade so fast?
Are they sad they didn't last?
I asked a daisy why it falls,
It just winked and said, 'The call.'

Do bees hum secrets in the air?
Or just buzz by without a care?
I chewed on grass to find their truth,
It tasted funny, like lost youth.

If rain makes puddles for kids to splash,
Do clouds get jealous of all the cash?
I pondered storms over my brunch,
But pancakes won and stole my lunch!

What if birds are just our dreams?
Flying high, or maybe it seems?
I tried to take flight and flopped instead,
Guess my wings are still in my head!

The Search for Light in Darkness

Why do we trip over unseen things?
Do shadows play games with our wings?
I fumbled around, looking for clues,
But found only dust and my old shoes.

If the moon's so bright, why hide from us?
Is it playing coy, just causing fuss?
I called out to it, 'Are you shy?'
But it just winked and passed me by.

In the dark, do stars host a party?
With twinkling lights, oh so hearty?
I tried to join up in their dance,
But tripped on a comet, lost my chance!

Why do we search for light in night?
Is it silly to think we might?
I held up my phone, full charge in hand,
And thought, "This flashlight's better planned!"

Wonderings of a Wandering Soul

If I roam the world looking for sense,
Will I find it in my neighbor's fence?
I asked the dog, who just barked back,
'The answers are in my snack pack!'

Why do we ponder when on the go?
Is the path a riddle wrapped in slow?
I chased a butterfly for a thrill,
But it flew off, and I took a spill.

Are clouds just thoughts from cosmic minds?
Drifting softly, no plans it finds?
I tried to catch one, failed, oh dear,
It laughed just like my last pint of beer!

If questions float like boats on the sea,
Do they sink if I shout, 'Let me be!'?
I launched my words, watched them drift away,
They took a holiday, what a cliché!

Existential Echoes

Why am I here, oh where's the map?
It seems my phone's dead, what a gap!
I trip on thoughts, while sipping tea,
Is this the end, or just a spree?

The stars above, like winking eyes,
Are they amused? Give me a prize!
I ponder deep, the cosmic play,
Did I leave the stove on? Oh, hooray!

I search for hints in daily grind,
Like socks that vanish, what's the kind?
Do ducks have dreams? What do they think?
Or do they just float, and sip the drink?

The clock keeps ticking, waits for none,
I might just nap, where's the fun?
So here's my laugh amidst the quest,
Just enjoy the ride, it's all a jest!

Fragments of Meaning

Why do we eat, and wear these shoes?
Who designed the chaos, and the blues?
With cereal hopes and milk for thought,
I find myself in webs I've caught.

The cat looks wise, while snoozing slow,
Does he hold secrets we don't know?
What's with the dust? Why does it cling?
Is it part of some grand old fling?

I count my coins, then lose my keys,
Dog barks loudly, curious breeze.
Are all my worries just illusions?
Or clever tricks and mad conclusions?

I'll chase the clouds, pretend to fly,
With ice cream dreams, we'll reach the sky.
Through giggles and gaffes we'll surely see,
The fun in questions, just let it be!

Tiny Whispers of Wisdom

What's the meaning of a blushing cat?
Is it just shy, or too much fat?
When fish can fly, we'll take a ride,
On thoughts of barbecue, side by side.

Why do pancakes always seem to flop?
Are they just teasing, or need a prop?
The toaster beeps, a subtle cue,
Is breakfast really worth the view?

With shoes untied and socks mismatched,
Life leans on me, a prank well hatched.
Are ducks in line to take a vote?
Or simply quacking for a boat?

I'll swing my worries with the breeze,
Past questions tangled in the trees.
So here's my jest, a giggle spry,
The tiny answers make me fly!

The Infinite and the Finite

The universe expands, or so they say,
But why's my room always in disarray?
The cosmos teases with endless charms,
While I dodge dust bunnies without alarms.

Is time a thief that steals our snacks?
As I ponder this, I lose my tracks.
With every tick, the clock's in jest,
Did I fridge the cake? Oh, what a test!

What's beyond the stars? Just more space?
Or is it all part of a cosmic race?
I sip my drink, and questions swell,
Is lemonade just a citrus spell?

I'll laugh as I chase the fleeting muse,
With hiccups and chuckles, who can refuse?
So raise a toast to nonsense divine,
For within the silly, wisdom will shine!

Contemplations from a Sunlit Window

Sipping tea with cosmic thoughts,
A squirrel mocks my grand ideas.
Do ducks have deep discussions?
Or just float on their feathery fears?

The clock ticks loud, like questions asked,
Of time and space, what makes us whole?
Is grass more green on the other side?
Or does it just play the fool on a roll?

A cat stares at the wall so blank,
Is it pondering secrets of the stars?
Or planning a coup against the fish?
I swear it knows all, behind those bars!

With every thought, I lose my track,
Should I chase the dream or chase the snack?
Answers hide like socks in the wash,
But the butter on toast brings laughter back.

Shadows of the Infinite

A shadow stretches long and wide,
Does it seek the truth or sun?
Maybe it's pondering what's inside,
Or just finding shade—a lazy run?

Is the universe really so vast?
Or just an endless game of 'hide and seek'?
Stars twinkle back with a wink and blast,
Or hide their secrets behind a peak?

Who's counting all the grains of sand?
Is each a dream lost from the tide?
Maybe they plot with a master plan,
Or just nap while the sun takes pride.

Oh, to ask the moon for advice,
But it just smiles in its silver glow.
Dear moon, are you wise or merely nice?
Or just a glowing orb with nowhere to go?

The Color of Uncertainty

What's the hue of a thought gone rogue?
Is it bright red or a gloomy gray?
Do colors burst like overripe rogue?
Or fade gently in a whispered sway?

If I paint my dreams in purple blush,
Will they dance like mad in sunlight's gleam?
Or will they just wallow in a hushed hush,
Like a half-baked plan that never steamed?

Chickens cross roads, with thoughts so bold,
What's it like to fly without wings?
Do they chuckle at humans, uncontrolled?
Or plot their escape to greater things?

Waves crash questions upon the shore,
Do they answer with foamy delight?
As my knowns dissolve, I seek some more,
And find my truths in the dead of night.

Musings of a Curious Heart

With a heart like a balloon, I float,
Where do dreams go when they deflate?
Do they gather in fields of hope?
Or pop like jokes left too late?

Questions spin like tops in the air,
Is there a manual for this crazy ride?
Do unicorns get lost in despair?
Or glide over puddles with pure pride?

I once asked a goldfish for advice,
But it just swam in its aquatic dance.
Maybe wisdom lies in being nice,
Or in letting each moment take a chance.

So here I sit, with queries unchained,
Giggling softly at the tales they spin.
In this wacky world, my heart remains,
Curious, playful, and ready to grin!

Patterns Revealed in Quiet Moments

In the midst of silence, I pause,
A donut's shape, life's great cause.
Patterns in sprinkles, all around,
In coffee stains, wisdom is found.

What's the secret to long-lost socks?
Hidden with keys in those junky boxes.
Questions arise, like bubbles in tea,
While cats plot world domination, you see!

The toaster hums tunes of bygone days,
As bread transforms in mysterious ways.
A dance with the butter, slick and spread,
Making light of crumbs, who needs that dread?

In quiet moments, fun takes the lead,
Making sense of nonsense, planting the seed.
Laughter bubbles up like soda so fizzy,
In life's riddle, it's all a bit dizzy!

Breaths Shared: The Pulse of Inquiry

Inhale the whispers, a chuckle, a sigh,
Why do we answer when the cat asks 'why'?
Every breath carries secrets unknown,
With popcorn kernels, wisdom is grown.

What's the weight of a feather, so light?
Or the tickle of truth in the moon's soft bite?
Balloons float questions to the sky,
While ants debate the meaning of 'why'.

A flick of the wrist, watch the clock chime,
Is it truly wise to measure in rhyme?
Conversations linger like jam on toast,
With laughter as music, we cherish the most.

In each shared breath, joy fills the space,
Curiosity dances with a quirky grace.
We ponder and wander, slight and amused,
As laughter and questions are brightly fused!

The Art of Embracing Mystery

A shadow's whisper and a light's embrace,
What's in my pocket? Oh, just a misplaced ace!
Mysteries twirl like socks in the wash,
Caught in the spin, they swish, then they slosh.

Why do plants lean when the sun calls,
While I trip on my words and stumble and fall?
A riddle unfolds like an origami tease,
As cookies crumble with effortless ease.

What is the recipe for clouds, I wonder?
Puffs of laughter, or lightning and thunder?
In each raindrop, a story awaits,
With puddles reflecting circus-like fates.

So here's to the questions, absurd yet profound,
In the art of mystery, joy can be found.
With giggles and wiggles, we chase the bizarre,
A dance with enigmas beneath the same star!

Light and Shadow: A Balancing Act

In the realm of shadows, the light softly sneaks,
Why do we trip on our own two feet?
A dance of opposites, tangled in fun,
Like cheese with potatoes, they're never outdone.

Why do we giggle at ghosts in the dark?
Their tales are just whispers, just missing the spark.
In laughter's embrace, the worries retreat,
With shadows as partners, we twirl on our feet.

The sun casts questions, a quirky parade,
Why do socks hop, while shoes seem afraid?
In reflecting on mischief, the joy overloads,
As laughter lights up the mysterious roads.

So balance your woes with a sprinkle of cheer,
In shadows and light, embrace what is near.
Questions are funny, though answers may lack,
In the dance of existence, we never look back!

A Breeze Through the Long Grass

Why do we run, when we can stroll?
Chasing our tails, that's our goal.
A bug flew by with a giggling sound,
Said, "Life's but a dance, just spin round!"

The sun shines bright, yet we wear shades,
Lost in the hues of life's charades.
A picnic laid, but ants take charge,
Tiny tyrants, they're living large!

Questions soar above like kites,
Tangled strings and playful flights.
While grasshoppers leap with glee,
Saying, "Why ask? Just be free!"

A feather falls, a gentle tease,
A reminder: just chill, if you please.
For who needs answers? Just take a pause,
And laugh at the whims of nature's laws.

The Tapestry of Unseen Connections

A cat and dog share a glance of fate,
Two worlds collide, oh isn't it great?
They ponder the depth of their shared space,
One licks a paw, the other, a face!

In crowded rooms, we dance unseen,
Knots in our hearts, like a big marionette fee.
Do we really know who we might spark?
Or is it just fate, sneaking through the dark?

A squirrel argues with a curious crow,
Over last night's leftover dough.
Questions scatter like petals in flight,
Chasing the breeze on a glimmering night!

Connections made through silly chatter,
More than just words, it's the joyful clatter.
Join the circus, throw out your fears,
For laughter's the thread that binds us here.

Searching for Answers in Starlight

Gazing up at the twinkling sky,
Wondering why the stars are shy.
"Do they blink at us?" I ask my friend,
She shrugs her shoulders, "What's the trend?"

A comet zooms, a brief delight,
"Is that my ex's car?" we laugh tonight.
Constellations giggle at our quest,
While we ponder how to rest.

Moons and planets in a cosmic dance,
While we trip and fall in a clumsy prance.
"Do they hear our woes?" we tilt our heads,
But the answer's a snore, as starlight spreads.

Napping stars whisper beneath their breath,
"Chasing questions? How quaint! Just let it rest."
With a wink and a shine, they twinkle bright,
And we join the dream, ready to take flight.

Beneath the Surface of the Ordinary

Underneath the mundane, joy resides,
Tickling the toes of our daily rides.
Why do we wear socks, when boots will do?
Fashion police giggle, 'What's wrong with you?'

A spoon bends low for a dance with a fork,
Creating chaos when people talk.
We ponder the fridge like it holds the key,
"What's in there?" While leftovers flee!

Indeed, the floor is a stage of clatter,
Dust bunnies join in, giving it matter.
What's the meaning of socks with stripes?
Just a giggle between the life types!

With giggles shared over clinking plates,
We seek magic in the simplest fates.
For in every crack and silly thing,
Lies a wonder that makes our hearts sing.

The Threads of Human Experience

Why do socks disappear in the wash?
It's a mystery, a cosmic nosh.
Lost in the spin, they dance away,
Making laundry day a comical play.

Is a hotdog a sandwich, or should it be?
As I ponder this while I sip my tea.
The universe shrinks with each tasty bite,
In this grand debate, everyone's right.

What's the point of Monday mornings, friend?
A cruel start, would you not defend?
Yet coffee brews like a wizard's charm,
Turning grumpy frowns into warm arms.

Do fish ever get thirsty through their gills?
If they do, what a dilemma it fills!
They swim and swim, but can't take a drink,
In the ocean of questions, we laugh and think.

Between the Lines of What is Known

Why do we step on cracks in the street?
It's a childhood habit, a dance with our feet.
Each step a gamble, a playful risk,
With every crunch, it's a silly brisk.

Do pigeons think they're the city's lords?
Cooing in rhythm, demanding their hoards.
While we walk by, they strut with pride,
Claiming the park as they glide and slide.

What happens when you make a wish?
Does it travel through stars or just end in a dish?
With every flickering candle's light,
We hope for magic to take flight.

Can a cat truly be an ancient sage?
With a stare that leaves one in a daze?
In their eyes lies a wit so divine,
Reminding us all, it's fine to recline.

Fleeting Echoes on the Edge of Infinity

If you forget where you put your keys,
Is it the universe playing with ease?
A cosmic joke or a funny tease,
Lost treasures hide, awaiting our pleas.

Why does chocolate magically mend a mood?
It's the sweet antidote to feeling crude.
With every bite, worries start to fade,
In the grand scheme, we're all just a parade.

Is there a limit to how deep one can dive?
In the pool of thoughts, we thrash to survive.
Splashing around in ripples of doubt,
We giggle while figuring what life's about.

Do pranksters in heaven laugh at our fate?
Telling jokes from a celestial gate?
With every twist, our stories unwind,
Leaving trails of laughter for us to find.

Beneath the Canopy of Uncertainty

Why does time always seem to fly?
One moment you're young, then goodbye!
As we age like cheese or fine wine,
We giggle at wrinkles that twist and twine.

Do aliens chuckle at Earthly quirks?
As we scroll through memes and random works.
In their distant ships, they sip their brew,
Wondering why we can't just be cool.

What's the secret to a well-baked pie?
Is it a dash of laughter or a wink in the eye?
With each slice served at the family feast,
The answers feel tiny, yet joy is increased.

Why do we seek answers at the stars?
When down here we're dancing with our own scars.
Under the moon's glow, we share and we sigh,
Choosing to laugh at our own alibi.

Fractals of Infinity

Why do socks disappear in a wash?
Are they plotting a grand escape?
Maybe they've joined a sock cult,
Dancing in the spin cycle's drape.

Do ants have tiny smartphones?
Texting friends about the crumbs?
With tiny screens they might be swamped,
But hey, they bring home all the crumbs!

If fish could talk, what would they say?
"Stop staring, we're just swimming here!"
But give them bread, they'll change their tune,
"More interest, please! We're quite sincere!"

What do clouds do when they're gray?
Maybe they're just in a mood.
Let's offer them a slice of pie,
And hope it lightens their attitude!

Small Answers to Big Wonders

What's the reason for a sneeze?
Is it just dust getting too bold?
A tiny sneeze is like a shout,
"Hey, I'm alive! Bring on the cold!"

Why do we forget where we park?
Sidewalks hide cars like a game.
We laugh and roam, then face the truth,
"Four wheels lost in a concrete frame!"

If a duck quacks, does it echo?
Or just ripple into the pond?
Does it ponder the meaning of quack,
Or simply swim on, completely abscond?

Are there aliens laughing at us?
Watching our clumsy earthly show?
With popcorn in hand, they shout, "Yay!",
As we trip on rocks, clueless below!

A Glimpse Through the Veil

Why do we yawn when we're tired?
Is it a signal to get some snooze?
Or a way to let others know,
"Coming soon, a nap I'll choose!"

Do fish look up and wonder why?
The sky is blue and not a sea.
"Is there food up there, or just a lie?
Let's dive down, it's safer, you see!"

Why are cats such good therapists?
With their purrs, they heal our souls.
Just a glance, and we forget cares,
They're fluffy magic in fur-filled rolls!

What makes the sun rise every day?
Does it have a schedule to keep?
"Morning again!" it beams with glee,
While we grumble and long for more sleep!

The Pulse of Now

What makes a tick-tock sound so loud?
Is it time laughing at our plight?
"Hey there, humans! Just a reminder,
You can't slow me down—what a delight!"

If toast could talk, what tales to tell?
"I'm golden crispy; don't eat me raw!"
With butter dreams and jammed-up thoughts,
They toast to life from their kitchen law.

Why do we trip and stumble so?
Is the floor out to pull us down?
Nope! It just loves our clumsy dance,
And we're the stars of the town!

If laughter's good medicine, you see,
Why are we sick, suffering fits?
Perhaps the joke's on all of us,
And the punchline's hidden in bits!

The Paradox of Small Wonders

Why do socks vanish, what an enigma,
A sockless dance party, oh what a stigma.
The cat stares at walls, like they hold great lore,
While I can't recall what I entered the room for.

The ants insist they know the route,
Yet I'm still puzzled by where my keys shoot.
A butterfly flaps, and chaos can reign,
While I ponder if my lunch will contain a grain.

The toast always lands with buttered side down,
As I'm left wearing crumbs like a quirky crown.
A sneeze at the wrong time can cause a great fuss,
Oh life's little quirks, they're amusing to us.

So here's to the riddles we giggle and chase,
In the mundane moments, we find our place.
We'll laugh at the mysteries, big and absurd,
For it's in tiny wonders our joy is stirred.

Fragments of a Cosmic Puzzle

Why is the moon so shy at noon?
Does it hide from the sun or just hum a tune?
Stars scattered like sprinkles on cosmic cake,
What do they think, for goodness' sake?

Is pizza a circle but served in a square?
Why does time fly when you're unaware?
Questions like bubbles that drift in the air,
Popping with laughter, a curious affair.

A spoon can't stop a soup's wild escape,
And jellybeans ponder their colorful shape.
Do fish ever dream of swimming on land?
Or wish for a life where they don't taste so bland?

In the fridge, do leftovers plot their revolt?
While we search for answers, a new snack to bolt.
Each inquiry's silly, let's not take a stand,
For puzzling's a game that we all understand.

Echoes of Unasked Queries

Why do we talk to ourselves in the mirror?
Is it the reflection that draws us much nearer?
Do plants feel our chatter, or just sit in the sun,
Wondering if their pot's really just for fun?

The toaster burns bread, it's not in its code,
Then winks as it serves us a breakfast road.
Are clouds just the cotton we forgot to fluff?
Why does the world insist on being so rough?

Socks on the wrong feet—what an odd twist,
Is it fashion or fate? Who can resist?
Why does the fridge hum like it's thinking deeply?
Or is it just waiting for us to eat cheaply?

In a cosmos so vast, do we really care,
If the answers are tiny, or simply unfair?
Let's embrace all the quirks, with laughter and cheer,
For unasked queries are what bring us near.

The Silence Between Thoughts

In the pause between bites, what do we seek?
Are we waiting for wisdom, or just feeling weak?
Do eyebrows raise questions, or merely frame eyes?
A silent conversation where mystery lies.

What happens to ice cubes after the drink?
Do they float off to sea for a long-life blink?
Do puns have emotions, or just aim to please?
Why do we laugh at the silliest tease?

Can shadows play tag when the sun's feeling bright?
Or do they just linger, avoiding the light?
What's the secret of tape that always gets lost?
Oh, the whims of our minds, not considering the cost.

In the still of the moment, we ponder and jest,
Finding delight in questions, we humorously nest.
So let's cherish the gaps, where nonsense can bloom,
For thoughts that go nowhere can lighten the room.

The Riddle of Time's Embrace

Why does a clock tick so fast?
Yet drags its feet on a Monday's cast?
I ponder why seconds feel like a tease,
While hours vanish like whispers in the breeze.

Do we treasure minutes, or let them flee?
As we sip coffee, lost in a sea?
Maybe the secret's tucked in the grind,
That time laughs just as we unwind.

They say time flies, yet sometimes it stalls,
Like waiting in line for those bathroom halls.
When will we learn, or will we just groan?
Perhaps the answer's just humorously known!

So dance with the clock and make it your friend,
For it bends, it twists, and it just might extend.
In the riddle of time, let's giggle and play,
As it shrinks and expands, come what may!

Gentle Reminders in Chasing Shadows

Why does the sun peek just at dawn?
While shadows linger, stretching till gone?
Chasing them down feels like a race,
But they vanish, leaving just empty space.

Whispering winds tease with cheerful delight,
They guide us to giggles in soft moonlight.
Why do we chase what we can't quite see?
Perhaps shadows just crave to be free!

We run after dreams like they're butterflies,
Yet they flutter away, much to our surprise.
But in chasing the fun, aren't we the prize?
As we laugh at our folly, under vast skies!

So here's to the dance in the light and the dark,
To the questions that chase us, leaving a mark.
For in every shadow, a smile can sprout,
And laughter's the victor that's never in doubt!

Patterns in the Chaos

Is there order in socks that collide?
Why is chaos where stripes like to hide?
In the circus of life, who holds the reins?
Perhaps the punchline lies in the stains!

With puzzle pieces all tossed around,
How do we find where meaning is found?
Like mismatched shoes in a closet so neat,
It seems we're still dancing to our own beat.

Do ants form lines, or is it just us?
As we ponder each step with a hint of disgust.
Perhaps the mess is where wisdom resides,
In the quirks of our nature, hilarity hides!

So let's embrace the delightful dismay,
For chaos is laughter in a sensible way.
With patterns unwrapped, let's jest and engage,
In the circus of living, turn each page!

The Weight of Simple Choices

Is it best to pick pizza or pie?
As ice cream rolls in, we surely sigh.
With each forkful, a decision we make,
Which flavor is best? Oh, for goodness' sake!

Should I wear blue jeans or choose a bright coat?
Every option's a wave in a whimsical boat.
Yet choosing a laugh can lighten the load,
While pondering whether to share the remote!

Who needs a map when roads all bend?
With choices like these, what's the end?
In the humor of choices we find that it's fair,
To let go of stress and breathe easy air!

So let's toast with our coffee, hearts all aglow,
For each choice we make turns into the show.
With joy at the helm, we'll sail through our fate,
In this merry-go-round, it's never too late!

Curiosity's Compass

Why are we here, just ask a cat,
They'll stare at you like you're a brat.
Exploring the fridge, they seek delight,
While we ponder why day turns to night.

Is coffee more magic than a spell?
Or just a trick our brains know too well?
In cups of mystery, we float and swirl,
Maybe there's wisdom in caffeine's whirl.

Do ducks discuss their pond plans neat?
Or are they just vibing, feeling the beat?
Questions like bubbles rise up to pop,
But laughter's the answer, so let's not stop!

So grab a snack, let worries go,
Under the sun's warm, golden glow.
With curiosity as our goofy map,
Let's enjoy the ride, and take a nap!

Shadows of Certainty

What if socks were meant to escape?
Those sneaky pairs, a true misshape.
In drawers they plot their great escape,
While we just chase their fuzzy drape.

Do clouds ever question their own fluff?
'Cause being so soft must get pretty tough!
Floating around with not much to do,
Making rain grumpy, or sunny skies blue.

Why do we laugh at our bad dad jokes?
Is it the punchlines or just the folks?
In moments of silence, there's always glee,
Even if 'who invited this joke?' is we.

So raise a toast to questions untold,
Embrace the absurdities, brave and bold.
In shadows of certainty, we'll dance and twirl,
Laughing while spinning in this crazy world.

Fleeting Thoughts on Eternity

If time had legs, where would it run?
Chasing after laughter and silly fun?
Would it stop for the ice cream truck,
Or get lost in a tick-tock muck?

What if stars blinked just to say hello?
Winking at us with a cosmic glow.
Would we dance in their sparkly light,
Or trip over shoelaces, oh what a sight!

Do ants hold meetings on a crumb?
Discussing their plans, all busy and dumb?
While we wonder if our thoughts are clear,
They strategize lunch, in perfect cheer.

In fleeting thoughts, let's celebrate now,
Forget the 'how' and the 'why' and the 'wow'.
For every giggle and wrinkled nose,
Isn't that what makes the best prose?

Moments Between the Stars

Can wishes run out, or just take a break?
What if they giggle, just to be fake?
One day a wish found a lost little sock,
Said, "I'm just here for a fun little walk!"

Do shadows romanticize the dark?
Or do they make plans just to leave a mark?
Whispering secrets, just out of sight,
Pondering life beneath the moonlight.

Why do we overthink all our snacks?
Should we really crunch or just cut some flack?
Potato chips or carrots in sight,
Every crunch feels like sheer delight.

So here's to moments, strange and bizarre,
Floating along on a tire swing star.
Let's relish the quirks, the laughs, and the sighs,
In this vast universe, we'll share all our highs!

A Universe of Unanswered Queries

Why do socks vanish in the wash?
Are they partying, or is it a ploy?
Where do the missing keys like to roam?
Perhaps they're on a quest for joy.

Is cereal a soup? That's a thought!
What's the speed of a sneeze, pray tell?
Do clouds ever worry they'll fall?
If they did, would they shout or just yell?

When will I find that perfect snack?
Is it hidden behind the TV?
Perhaps it smiles back with its crunch?
Yet all I find is a sad old pea.

Oh, where do all the good times go?
Do they dance off with yesterday's sun?
I'd trade a few for a fresh donut,
But I fear those calories might run!

The Fragile Thread of Certainty

If I make a plan, will it hold?
Or will it wiggle like a worm?
The more I think, the less I'm sure,
But hey, uncertainty's got charm!

Is it fate that gives me this hair?
Each strand a question, a curious curl?
Maybe the universe laughs at my locks,
A giggle at my tangled world!

Why does ice cream melt so fast?
It's a leak of joy, not just a treat.
I chase it down with a plastic spoon,
But gravity always claims defeat!

What's the secret of a good dad joke?
Is it timing or just pure luck?
I ponder these things with a grin,
And groan when I hear my own chuck!

Can socks and dreams ever match?
I've tried, but those socks just don't play.
Perhaps life's just meant to be odd,
And laughter's the best game to stay!

Questions Like Raindrops

Why are there clouds in a blue sky?
Do they plan a parade, or just float?
Do raindrops gossip just like us?
Or do they have deeper thoughts to note?

What if trees could speak their minds?
Would they share tales of the birds?
Perhaps they'd tell us of the winds,
And laugh at our silly human words.

Is every hiccup a playful ghost?
Or a quirk from my lunch in a race?
My body's a puzzle of strange tunes,
A concerto of chaos in space!

Do ants have meetings when I'm not there?
A secret society to discuss?
They march in lines like a business crew,
But never invite me – how rude, just!

If laughter's a currency, can I be rich?
With pockets full of chuckles to share?
Each giggle a gem, each snort a find,
A treasure stored with too much flair!

In Search of the Unseen

What's hiding behind that closed door?
A monster, a friend, or just some shoes?
Are there secrets waiting to be found?
Or just last week's laundry with no clues?

Is the universe listening to our thoughts?
If it is, I hope I sound cool!
Do stars roll their eyes at my dreams?
Or do they giggle like it's a school?

Can my pet understand my woes?
Or is he just waiting for a snack?
Perhaps he's pondering his own purpose,
Like a squirrel on a quest for a cracker pack!

Am I the punchline of fate's big joke?
Or just a clown in a cosmic gig?
Life's a circus, that much I know,
With laughter and wonders, oh so big!

The Ephemeral Beauty of Questions

Why does toast always land spread side down?
It's a mystery wrapped in a golden-brown gown.
Do socks have a secret life in the wash?
Perhaps they dance freely, making a swash!

Is the goldfish truly pondering the deep?
Or singing a tune while we're off to sleep?
When you lose your keys, where do they go?
Maybe they frolic in a world we don't know!

Are the shadows just playing a trick on the light?
Or are they on strike, avoiding the bright?
Why do we ask if the chicken saw grass?
Was it a plan that just didn't come to pass?

In the end, the answers might give us a grin,
Or leave us confused, caught in a spin.
But let's toast to questions, big and small,
For in their silliness, we can find it all!

Lighthouses in Stormy Seas of Doubt

In the storm of thoughts, why is it so bright?
Are the worries just cans in an old-fashioned fight?
If life's a puzzle, am I missing a piece?
Or just rearranging for a moment of peace?

Do ducks waddle for fun or just to impress?
Is each awkward step part of a grand process?
Why do we ponder what's behind the doors?
Are we afraid of monsters or just bored with chores?

When the tides of doubt crash against our shores,
Do we build little boats or just hide in drawers?
And when we trip on our own two feet,
Is it the universe laughing or just a funny feat?

In the waves of confusion, we search for a guide,
But sometimes it feels like we're just along for the ride.
Still, let's hoist the sails and enjoy the show,
For laughter's our lighthouse in the ebb and flow!

The Movement of Thought in Still Waters

In the pond of reflect, do frogs think aloud?
Or are their thoughts quiet, like a curious crowd?
Why do we ponder the roots of a tree?
Is it the answer to 'who' and 'what' and 'me'?

Do clouds ever wonder what it's like to be?
Or do they just drift with no thought or glee?
When we sulk in silence, what do we see?
Perhaps just the snacks waiting patiently!

Why does the sun rise and set on this sphere?
Is it a dance we all miss or a sight we revere?
And when we're stuck, what should we pursue?
Do thoughts hit rewind, or are they brand new?

As we ponder our thoughts, like ripples they spread,
Each question a snack that's gently been fed.
So here's to the moments of stillness and cheer,
For in the murmur of 'why', our fun will appear!

A Symphony of Whys and Hows

Why do we laugh at the silliest things?
Do the giggles take flight on invisible wings?
How does a cat always find the warm spot?
Is it a magic trick or just a good plot?

Why do we argue over pineapple on pie?
Is it culinary sin, or are we just shy?
When we look for answers beneath the old moon,
Do the stars just chuckle and hum a sweet tune?

How come the toast often pops like a clown?
Is it craving applause when it lands upside down?
Why does the grass tickle our bare little toes?
Is it teasing us lightly, or simply it knows?

In this symphony of whys, the laughter resounds,
With each funny question, the joy knows no bounds.
Let's waltz with our doubts and dance through the day,
For humor's the music that shows us the way!

The Weight of Each Breath

Why does the cat sit on the mat?
He ponders deep thoughts or naps like that.
Is seven hours sleep a universal need?
Or just an excuse to skip the dog's feed?

The scale tips funny with chocolate cake,
Do calories count when you're wide awake?
Do socks disappear in the dryer's embrace?
Or do they just run off to a happier place?

Why does my phone always lose my calls?
Yet captures my selfies in glittery stalls?
Is it magic or just mind's twisted scheme?
Perhaps my phone is living a dream?

So I juggle my thoughts as I juggle my weight,
Is wisdom found in my terrible fate?
With each breath I take, I ponder and grin,
Is the secret to joy where the chaos begins?

Mysterious Chimes of Existence

Why do ducks quack in a neat little row?
Are they discussing which pond they'll go?
Does the moon feel lonely up there in the sky,
When the stars blink back like they're saying hi?

Do plants gossip when no one is near?
Or just wave hi in their leafy sphere?
Is laughter the glue that sticks us so tight,
Or just a quick fix for a silly midnight?

What's the secret code of the universe vast?
Is it hidden in shadows or simple and fast?
Do ants have meetings we'll never attend,
Discussing their plans and how they can blend?

So I dance with the questions, upbeat and spry,
With whimsical thoughts that will soar and fly.
Perhaps each riddle is meant just for fun,
Or the giggle we find when the day's almost done!

The Mirror of Every Day

Is my hair a masterpiece or just a big mess?
When I look in the mirror, it's hard to guess.
Do socks have feelings when they lose their mate?
Is the toaster plotting with the plate?

Why do I trip over flat surfaces too?
Gravity must have a vendetta on you!
Do shoes conspire during a rainy spree,
To make me slip like I'm on a TV spree?

Does the coffee know how much it's adored?
Or does it weep quietly when I am bored?
Is there a debate at the breakfast table,
Between eggs and toast on who's more stable?

So I dance with reflections, each day a delight,
With giggles and snickers from morning till night.
In the mirrors of moments, through laughter we glide,
Finding joy in the chaos, right here by our side!

Threads of Curiosity in the Loom of Time

If time's a sweater, why's it so frayed?
Did I pull a thread or is that just fate?
What do fish think in their watery home?
Do they dream of land, or prefer to roam?

Why do we argue with strings of our fate?
As if we could change it with silly debate?
Does a butterfly giggle when it's caught in the breeze?
Or is it just checking how to land with ease?

Are clouds just cotton candy of the skies?
Do they giggle and dance as they twist and rise?
Why do we wonder about trivial things,
As if the answers come with invisible wings?

So I weave my questions, a tapestry bright,
With jests and with ponderings that ignite delight.
In the loom of existence where humor aligns,
We stitch the absurd, threading through our designs!

Sips of Wisdom from a Cracked Cup

In a café, wisdom brews,
Like coffee with too much snooze.
Ask the barista, he might know,
Why socks vanish, where do they go?

Spilled thoughts stain the table's cloth,
Is it fate, or just my sloth?
A cookie crumbles with a care,
Tastes like answers—beyond compare!

Muffins whisper secrets sweet,
While croissants dance on tiny feet.
Who needs a guide, a map, a plan?
When pastry's wisdom is at hand?

So take a sip, embrace the chance,
Life's trials may lead to a funny dance.
With a cracked cup, we toast and cheer,
For nonsense is wisdom when we steer!

The Dance of Hope and Hesitation

On a stage, two feet will prance,
Hope leads in a clumsy dance.
Hesitation taps a cautious beat,
Will this rhythm be a treat?

Life's questions twist and twirl,
In skirts of doubt, they swirl.
Yet laughter bubbles in the air,
As we trip without a care.

Twirl again, oh joyful chance,
Embrace the wobbly, silly dance.
With every turn, we find a laugh,
As purpose hides in half a gaffe.

So take a step, let worries break,
Spin with joy for your own sake.
For in the dance of hope and fear,
Lies the adventure we hold dear!

Piecing Together Fragments of Truth

In a puzzle box, truths collide,
Some fit well, some slide aside.
With each piece, a giggle erupts,
Gluing nonsense and dreams in supped-ups.

A corner missing—what a tease!
Is it laughter or just unease?
I swear I had that golden piece,
It vanished, oh the sweet deceit!

Let's join the bits, both big and small,
Each odd shape—the joy of it all!
When nonsense fits where logic tried,
We laugh and toss our doubts aside.

So grab your pieces, every shade,
In their chaos, memories played.
Fragmented truths, they shine quite bright,
In a game where all's delight!

Eyes Wide Open: The Great Unraveling

With eyes wide, we gaze and see,
The world's a wacky jubilee!
Threads unravel with each new tale,
As life's fabric's oddly frail.

A sock parade, or so it seems,
Each thread tangled with our dreams.
Questions dance like fairies light,
In the glow of the moon at night.

What's the secret? What's the score?
The punchline knocks, we laugh for sure.
With every twist, a grin appears,
For doubts dissolve with joyous cheers.

So let the unraveling commence,
With laughter, paints bright in the tense.
For clarity may come and go,
But fun? That's the real show!

Scribbles of Wonder on a Blank Page

Why does the cat stare, eyes wide and bright?
Is it plotting my downfall or just a late-night fright?
The sock on the floor, it must hold a clue,
To universe secrets we never quite knew.

Do ants have a plan when they march in a line?
Or do they just wander, sipping on wine?
The fridge hums a tune, does it dream of a pie?
Or is it just singing to the vegetables nearby?

A sneeze sends confetti across the dull room,
Is it just a reaction, or an impromptu bloom?
Maybe my coffee is plotting to spill,
While I ponder my purpose and roast on the grill.

With crayons I doodle my fears and my care,
Each scribble, a question, each swirl, a dare.
What if the paper responds to my call,
And reveals all the answers I missed in my fall?

The Significance of Small Things

In a world made of giants, what's up with the ants?
Do they dance at their picnics, or are they just chants?
The pebble on my shoe, is it heavy with fate?
Or just a tiny nuisance I should eliminate?

A sneeze could start thunder, or rain from the sky,
Is it really a blessing, or merely a sigh?
The sock that goes missing, does it join a parade?
While I search every closet, feeling betrayed.

Why do spoons seem so shiny while forks just look grim?

Is it all in the attitude, or did spoons just swim?
The cookie that crumbled, was it sick of the load?
Or just seeking freedom down the crumbly road?

With a sigh of the couch, and a grin from the chair,
I ponder small objects hiding without care.
The meaning of dust bunnies, do they plot or just play?
In this curious universe, they brighten my day.

Navigating the Ocean of Possibilities

A spoon in the ocean, what treasure will gleam?
Navigating waves like I'm lost in a dream.
Do fish hold a map drawn in scales on their back?
Or do they just wiggle, in an ocean of snack?

What if the jellyfish have blankets in tow?
And sip on the currents all to and fro?
The waves whisper secrets to shells on the beach,
But I still can't hear them, oh, what do they teach?

Do the clouds trade their shapes in a stormy chess game?
Or are they just drifting, feeling no shame?
The sunset's a painter with colors to fling,
While seagulls make music, oh what joy they bring!

Each splash of the wave, a riddle to solve,
As I drift through the shallows, my worries dissolve.
Perhaps I'm the captain of a ship made of laughs,
Setting sail on a sea full of whimsical paths.

Journeys Beyond the Horizon of Thought

Do thoughts wear their shoes when they're out on a stroll?

Or do they prefer slippers while guarding my soul?
The pink elephant pirouettes in my mind,
With tutus of clouds, it's something I find.

Do questions float by like balloons in the air?
Or are they more like kittens, seeking a dare?
The tickles of giggles, where do they all roam?
Do they find little corners and make them a home?

The moon croons a lullaby to the stars,
While I nibble on dreams from my sweet candy jars.
Is cheese really wisdom, or just a fun joke?
Or do mice hold the answers, in whispers bespoke?

In the journey of brainwaves, each twist and each bend,
What if these musings just never should end?
So let's skip on the pathways of curious thought,
For the dance of ideas is what we've all sought!

www.ingramcontent.com/pod-product-compliance
Lightning Source LLC
Chambersburg PA
CBHW051643160426
43209CB00004B/773